Champagne Travel Guide

Sightseeing, Hotel, Restaurant & Shopping Highlights

Jason Russell

Table of Contents

French Champagne Region

Tantalizing vineyards stretching over 34,000 hectares make for a strong first impression when visiting *La Champagne*. This is just the start of a bubbly love affair. Champagne – a historic French province of great natural beauty, 160 kilometers east of Paris – has a long-standing tradition in viticulture dating from the first century.

Indeed, there is no other place in the world where one is legally allowed to make a drink and call it 'champagne'; it is only here, in the homeland of the luxury sparkling white wine that all the required conditions are being met.

These include the maritime fossils in the chalky soil, the favorable climate and the undulating landscape. In fact, the name Champagne is derived from the Latin *campania* and denotes the similarity of the rolling hills to the Italian *Campania* countryside south of Rome.

Travelers will undoubtedly be mesmerized by the cavernous chalk tunnels stretching for hundreds of kilometers under the modern cities of Reims and Epernay. Some of these are over 30 meters deep and date back to ancient Roman times when inhabitants were searching for material from which to build their cities.

The tunnels are nowadays called *crayeres* and act as cellars for millions of bottles of precious champagne. Above ground, one can't help but flock to the large champagne *maisons* or to the smaller and more intimate estates of the *vignerons* (small cultivators) where hours upon hours of tasting can be a very enjoyable way to spend your days.

The 220-kilometer-long Champagne Roads (*Routes Touristique de Champagne*) are intertwined between the triangle formed by 3 cities: Reims, Epernay and Chateau-Thierry. These routes divide the region into four sections of Champagne vineyards: the *Massif de Saint-Thierry* northwest of Reims, the *Valle de la Marne* found on the road south of Reims and towards Epernay, the gorgeous *Montagne de Reims* east of Epernay and the *Cote de Blancs* - the Chardonnay cradle just south of Epernay.

Some 80 very proud producers can be found along the routes and many of them will welcome you warmly into their houses and show you the unparalleled wine heritage and tradition of the region.

The sparkling drink is the most likely reason travelers visit Champagne though the area has quite a few other aces up its sleeve, including an undisputed significance in French history, spectacular World Heritage Sites and a delectable cuisine. And even though present-day Champagne is generally known as the home of the world's most glorious golden drink, the primary significance of the province until the 19th century stemmed from its importance as a de-facto center of French crowning events.

Thread around Reims to comprehend the magnitude of the city's heritage before moving on to exploring the bubbles and other delightful treats that the Champagne region has to offer.

Culture

The culture of the region is steeped in champagne as it was here that the sparkling wine was first produced around 1700. Centuries preceding this historical event were marked by the coronation festivities held here regularly, further adding to the general feel of luxury, nobility and royalty around the Champagne. Quite understandably, it is both the region's legacy as a royal setting and the careful marketing of champagne as a drink of prestige associated with celebrations that has given Champagne a distinct affluent feel.

But only immersing in the daily champagne-production culture will certainly limit you from finding out more about some of the most important French heritage deeply rooted in Champagne. Let the Reims Cathedral dazzle you with its stained glass, marvel at the flamboyant robes worn by French kings at the Palais du Tau and delight at the wood engravings by Durer at the Le Verguer Museum. Reims indeed is the culture capital of the region and a very important city in the history of France; beyond the many coronations it was also the site of surrender when the German army waved the white flag here in 1945.

Despite its historic importance and status, Champagne is not snobbish. The warm and friendly people will welcome you into their truly remarkable homeland and honor you with their traditional hospitality, tempting cuisine and a glass full of bubbly.

Location & Orientation

Getting to Champagne is easy; the A4 and A26 motorways serve the region quite well but super-fast (TGV) trains are also a good option as they speed like bullets, cutting down on travel time across vast France. A TGV journey from Paris to Reims, for example, takes no more than 45 minutes and justifies the selection of Paris as the most common point of arrival by air.

Though public transportation is regular and convenient for moving between regional cities, having a car does provide the advantage of flexibility and ease of visiting more remote areas and smaller rural villages. However, trains and buses readily connect most cities and villages and distances around the region are often small.

When you have explored your most likely starting point of Reims, make a detour and head to Verzenay to check out the strange vineyard lighthouse then step into champagne heaven as you move towards Hautevillers, Epernay and Ay. From Epernay, consider making a day-trip to industrial Troyes with its multiple shopping outlet centers.

Climate & When to Visit

The climate in Champagne is quite variable but winters are typically cold and clear while summers are usually warm and dry. Any time between May and October would be a good choice for a visit to the region, though the fall harvest period is typically preferred both for the superior weather and for the chance to experience the annual event of greatest importance in this part of France.

If you do visit during the warmer summer months, you'll likely find yourself spending more time than usual in the dark and cool chalk cellars even though average temperatures in July are generally comfortable around 24 °C (75 °F). Do keep in mind that even though July and August are popular months to visit Champagne, the crowds are in no way comparable to other regions in France which are bustling in the summertime.

The months between November and April are best avoided because many champagne houses are closed for the first few months of each year, as are some hotels and restaurants.

Sightseeing Highlights

Reims

Reims is Champagne's metropolis; a walkable city of around 200,000 inhabitants with impressive French history landmarks sitting on top of millions of bottles of champagne fermenting underground. This rich mix of the availability of the golden liquid, multiple World Heritage Sites and a cosmopolitan and vibrant city atmosphere all make Reims a logical choice as a starting point on the Champagne trail. It is also a very accessible city; high-speed trains link Reims with many other French cities, including Paris, Bordeaux, Lille and Nantes.

Reims dates from Roman times and has a legacy of a glorious past but was largely destroyed during WWI. Today's city was mostly rebuilt in the Art Nouveau and Art Deco style during the 1920s, with tree-lined avenues and elegant squares. Even though it is pedestrianized to a great degree, the public bus system is the best method for navigating the city – buses are reliable, regular and generally a good value (€1 for one ride to anywhere in the city, €8.60 for a carnet of 10 tickets, €3 for a day pass).

Because the city is so steeped in history, it is easy to forget the fact that this is champagne heaven. Reims is in fact where most of the big champagne-producing houses are located or at least have their offices. Tastings and tours are organized in most and provide a glimpse into the chalk caves underground.

Generally, it is a good idea to pre-book champagne houses' tours in Reims although there are some houses that allow non-appointment visits, worth mentioning among these are Lanson (lanson.fr; tours from €15) and Taittinger (taittinger.fr; €16). Few houses worth booking in advance of your Reims visit include G.H.Martel & Co (champagnemartel.com; €11), Mumm (www.mumm.com; from €10) and Veuve Clicquot (veuve-clicquot.com; €25).

Notre Dame de Reims

Place du Cardinal Luçon 51100 Reims
Tel: +33 3 26 47 55 34
http://www.cathedrale-reims.com/

The massive 13th century *Notre Dame de Reims* is the city's most popular feature and France's historic coronation venue. It was here, in one of Europe's most magnificent buildings from the Middle Ages, that pompous ceremonies were held to celebrate the crownings of 33 French sovereigns over the course of a millenium.

This practice started even before the Notre Dame was built as the structure that stood there before the Cathedral provided the setting for the baptism of Clovis, the King of Franks, in the 5th century – an event that essentially marked the birth of the French Kingdom. But perhaps the most important ceremony ever to have taken place in this historic structure was the legendary coronation of Charles VII in 1429, lead by Joan of Arc.

Today a UNESCO World Heritage Site and renowned for its height (38m in the very center) this late Gothic cathedral in the heart of Reims was begun in 1211 and finished one century later. It has a very intricate west façade with three portals featuring carvings inspired by scenes from the Bible as well as a north door with a *Smiling Angel* statue, just one of the 2,303 fascinating statues that adorn this Cathedral. Stained glass windows from various periods can be observed in the nave and choir.

One of the windows (the south transept one) was done by the local Jacques Simon in 1954 and portrays Dom Perignon, the monk whose name frequently linked to the invention of champagne. Other notable features include the Gothic organ case with the Christ figure on top, the 15th century astronomical clock and the windows done by Marc Chagall in 1974. If 250 steps sound like something you may want to do, the Cathedral 15th century 81-meter-high tower (and roof) is yet another place to visit in the Notre Dame de Reims.

The most attractive angle from which to approach the Notre Dame is via rue Libergier, from the west. Entry into the Cathedral costs €7.50 (free for those under 26) while tickets for combined visits to the Cathedral and the nearby Palais de Tau cost €11. The Notre Dame de Reims is open from 07:30 to 19:30 daily with the exception of Sunday morning during Mass. Guided tours are available at multiple scheduled times throughout the day.

Palais du Tau

2 Place du Cardinal Luçon
51100 Reims
Tel: +33 3 26 47 81 79
http://palais-tau.monuments-nationaux.fr/

The second World Heritage Site in Reims is the Gothic *Palais du Tau*, a former archbishops' residence located next to the Cathedral. Its name derives from the building plan, resembling the letter T (*tau* in the Greek alphabet) and its oldest part – the chapel - dates from 1207. The Palais was rebuilt in the Gothic style in the early 16th century but was given its current Baroque appearance in the late 17th and early 18th centuries.

It used to be the residence of French princes right before their coronations and the venue of the crowning banquets which were held in the tapestry-decorated Tau Room. Organized as a museum in present times, it holds a treasure of items previously found in the Notre Dame, including statues, magnificent tapestries, robes and liturgical objects most of which are displayed in the Great Hall (*Salle de Tau*). The royal treasury is the home of the Charlemagne talisman from the 9th century and the Saint Remi chalice from the 12th century. Head to the second floor of the Palais for spectacular views of the Notre Dame.

The Palais is open from 09:30 to 12:30 and from 14:00 to 17:30 September to May and from 09:30 to 18:30 during the other months. It is closed on Mondays. Admission costs €7.50 (free for those under 26). A restaurant can be found on the premises.

Basilique St-Remi

Place du Chanoine Ladame 51100 Reims
Tel: +33 3 26 85 31 20
http://stremi-reims.cef.fr/

This 11th century former Benedictine church – the oldest in the city - completes the trio of World Heritage Sites in Reims and is a curious mix of the Romanesque and the Gothic. Named in honor of Bishop Remi (who, in 498, baptised Clovis in the basilica preceding the Notre Dame), it features a chandelier with 96 candles, one for each year of his life.

The origins of the Church lie in the 6th century chapel dedicated to Saint Christopher. Abbot Aviard took on the ambitious project of rebuilding the church in the early 11th century only to see the vaulting collapse some 2 decades later. It was in the middle of that century that the current basilica was finally erected by Abbot Theodoric.

Just like in the Notre Dame, impressive stained glass can be found in the St-Remi as well as a grand organ. The Romanesque nave of the church leads to a choir with pointed arches. The Bishop's tomb is also located inside the Basilica, elaborately carved with figures and columns. Visiting it was a part of every French coronation ceremony.

To get to the Basilica, use bus A or F, stop St-Remi. Another sight of interest nearby is the next-door *Musee St-Remi* - a museum focusing on archeology and military history. The St-Remi is open from 08:00 to 19:00 and admission is free. Admission to the museum costs €4.

Musee de la Reddition

12 Rue du Président Franklin Roosevelt,
51100 Reims
Tel: +33 3 26 47 84 19

This military-themed museum, dubbed Museum of the Surrender (*Musee de la Reddition*), showcases the former US General Eisenhower's well-preserved headquarters completely covered with Allied maps, uniforms, documents and photographs all focused around a single date - May 7th, 1945, the day when Nazi Germany under General Jodl surrendered to the Allied forces thus marking the end of WWII.

The small but nevertheless moving room where the documents were signed remains precisely as it was. A short film screening tells the story of the important date and marks the start of the guided tour of the Museum.

The Museum is open from 10:00 to 12:00 and from 14:00 to 18:00 daily except on Tuesdays. Entrance is free on the first Sunday of every month and on May 8th; regular admission costs €4. The Museum can be accessed via bus line 4, stop Roosevelt.

Musee Hotel Le Vergeur

36 Place du Forum,
51100 Reims
Tel: +33 3 26 47 20 75
http://www.museelevergeur.fr/

A townhouse used between the 13th and 16th century, the *Musee Hotel Le Vergeur* provides excellent insight into period architecture and interior design. Built during the 13th century in a mix of late medieval and early Renaissance styles, it was the home to a number of aristocrats and champagne traders and was later acquired by Hugues Kraft who was a local art patron intent on preserving Reims' historic buildings.

Rooms open to visitors include a smoking room and Napoleon III's bedroom while a spectacular Renaissance façade and 15th century original engravings by Albrecht Durer (including *The Apocalypse* and *Great Passion*) are also of interest to art-lovers.

The Museum is open from 14:00 to 18:00 every day except Monday and admission costs €5 for adults. Guided tours are available every hour on the hour. The Museum can be accessed by Citadines bus line 1 or 2, stop Forum.

Porte de Mars

Place de la République,
51100 Reims

The massive Porte de Marse is a triumphal gate with three arches dating from the early 3rd century and is Reims' oldest monument. It gave access to the Gallo-Roman town of *Durocrtorum* and was the widest arched gate in Roman times. The central arch was used for carts while the two side arches for pedestrian traffic. Original sculptures can still be observed on it, including those of Romulus and Remus, Leda and the swan. It is 32 meters long and 13 meters high and served as a city gate until 1544.

Musee des Beaux-Arts

8 Rue Chanzy, 51100 Reims
Tel: +33 3 26 35 36 00

A spectacular collection awaits travelers in the Fine Arts Museum (*Musee des Beaux-Arts*) in Reims: four versions of Jacque-Louis David's *The Death of Marat*, many works by Camille Corot as well as a dozen of German Renaissance portraits by the Cranachs are just some of the treasures worth noting.

Masterpieces by Monet, Gauguin and Pissaro can also be found inside this Museum located a short distance from the Notre Dame and housed in an 18th century building, formerly the Abbey of St. Denis. Visitors should note that this 1794-founded museum is currently only open for temporary exhibitions and scheduled to fully reopen in all its glory in 2017 when it will be located in new premises.

The Fine Arts Museum is open from 10:00 to 12:00 and from 14:00 to 18:00 daily; closed on Tuesdays. Entrance is free on the first Sunday of every month; admission tickets cost €3 for the temporary exhibitions and €6 for the temporary and permanent exhibitions. Bus lines 2, 4 and 5 (stop Rockefeller) make for easy access to the Museum.

Verzenay

As you head from Reims to Epernay, a slight detour some 15 kilometers to the southeast of Reims makes for a pleasant half-day trip. The small village of Verzenay (population 1,100) lies within the *Montegne de Reims* and its vineyards are classified as Grand Cru - 100% - Pinot Noir. But the most notable highlight of Verzenay is its lighthouse (*Phare de Verzenay*) which houses a Champagne museum. It is entirely unusual to find a lighthouse set on a hilltop amidst vineyards but the structure was built as a publicity gimmick in 1909 by Champagne J. Goulet with the goal of promoting champagne.

Declining into oblivion after the severe destruction suffered during WWI, the lighthouse was rescued by the municipality of Verzenay in the 1980s, restored and then converted into a museum (*Musee de la Vigne*). A total of 101 spiral stairs take visitors to the top of the lighthouse from where spectacular views of the vineyards can be enjoyed.

The museum inside the lighthouse, opened in 1999, outlines the history of champagne, its production process as well as the geology of the region's soil through a 90 minute tour combining movies, instruments and models. The Museum is open every day except Monday from 10:00 to 17:00. Admission costs €7.50 while a combined visit to both the lighthouse and museum cost €8.50. A ticket for a visit to the lighthouse only costs €3.

Hautevillers

Before arriving into Epernay, make sure you make a stop in the small but very historic town of Hautevillers, only about 5 kilometers north of Epernay. This hillside town was the home of Dom Perignon, a blind Benedictine monk with extraordinary taste buds and sense of smell. Perignon, born in 1639, blended wines from various vineyards and in a way 'invented' champagne.

Truth be told, the refermentation of wine was only able to be controlled from the 18th century onwards but the monk's champagne legacy remains nevertheless and he is still remembered as an oenologist ahead of his time.

Wander around Hautevillers' streets and marvel at the wrought iron signs that tell the story of the town. Follow them recount their stories, including the one revolving around champagne's production.

To pay homage to Dom Perignon, head to the Hautvillers' church where he is buried. The Church also features a museum, reconstructing Dom's cellar and laboratory, and provides a glimpse into the life of one of the region's most beloved figures.

Epernay

Some 25 kilometres south of Reims on the left bank of the Marne River and easily accessible by train, Epernay is Reims' main champagne rival and a town almost religiously devoted to the sparkling wine. Though Reims is larger, Epernay is the more likely real center of champagne's production as it lies at the intersection of three vineyard regions (Montagne de Reims, Cote des Blancs and Marne).

The town is also a good choice to base yourself in should you decide to visit Champagne during the harvest (end of August to mid September) given the proximity of the vineyards. Surrounded by scenic vine-covered hills, it is the home of many champagne houses.

Visitors undoubtedly march to the famous *Avenue de Champagne* (once named 'the most drinkable street in the world' by Churchill), lined with champagne *maisons* located in 18th and 19th century houses. The charm of Eperney lies in the ease and accessibility of champagne along the avenue; travelers can freely float from one to the other for a day of bubbly fun.

Most of the houses have public tours on weekdays and some even on weekends and the prices for such tours start at about €5. The most notable trio of houses includes *Moet et Chandon*, *Mercier* and *De Castellane*, each one offering a somewhat different take on a tour which invariably ends with visitors sampling a glass (or few) of the world's most sought-after bubbles.

Perhaps the most famous one and definitely the largest of these is **Moet et Chandon** (20 Ave de Champagne, http://www.moet.com/). The year 1741 was a historic point in time for Epernay when Moet (now Moet et Chandon) founded the first champagne house and essentially turned the art of champagne making into an industry. The LVMH Empire (owning Louis Vuitton, Moet and Hennessy) is the ultimate in prestige and luxury.

The Moet champagne was preferred by Napoleon who was rumoured to drink cases of it before each battle. Moet provides a somewhat generic tour of their house and 28 kilometers of tunnels, featuring a video as well as a taste-test of their champagne. Prices at this luxury-centered cellar start at around €15 per tour with one tasting.

Mercier (68 Ave de Champagne, http://www.champagnemercier.fr/), today at the lower end of the price range of champagnes, is true to M. Mercier's goal of making champagne more accessible to everyday people and provides an interesting tour including a visit to a giant oak barrel. The history of the Mercier champagne is truly fascinating and the caverns underground are explored through a laser-guided train.

The cellars at Mercier are definitely the longest in all of Epernay as Mercier himself decided to build an underground town and aimed to connected it to the Paris-Strasbourg railway line. Mercier's personality was as interesting as his champagne; he even transported the world's largest champagne barrel full of vintage bubbly all the way to Paris during the Universal Exhibition. A guided visit with three tastings at Mercier starts at €18.

The third house, **De Castellane** (63 Ave de Champagne, http://www.castellane.com/), provides a tour of the cellars, the modern assembly lines and the vat that hold the juice before fermentation. A small museum can also be found on the estate and showcases traditional winemaking instruments. Part of the tour is the sweaty climb to the top of De Castellane's 66-meter-high tower, an exact copy of the Gare de Lyon clock-tower in Paris.

Each house also provides the option of purchasing bottles in their end-of-tour boutiques and though prices are pretty standard, some houses do provide discounts. If you are strapped for time and money and want to see a wide selection of affordable champagne from independent producers, head to the **C.Comme Champagne** on rue Gambetta (more details can be found in the Shopping section of this guide).

Ay

Some 5 kilometers east of Epernay, the small Grand Cru village of Ay (4,200 inhabitants) is known as the champagne production center and its wines have been recorded as early as the first century AD.

Ay is famous for its bi-annual champagne festival (Festival of Henry IV) taking place during the first weekend in July of every even-numbered year. A parade, tastings, exhibitions, fireworks and other events provide entertainment to some 25,000 visitors during each festival. It is a relaxed and casual village that remains open and friendly even during the busy festival days.

The town provides no more than a handful of restaurants and bars but it is the select location of over 20 champagne houses owning vineyards nearby including Bollinger, Deutz & Gelderman, Ayala and Gosset, so touring few more houses here may be a good idea. But perhaps one of the most interesting activities available to visitors of Ay is the guided vineyards' tour in an electric car. The 2-hour long tour provides an ecological method of visiting the vineyards and includes a champagne tasting right among the grapes. For more information, visit http://www.ay-eco-visite.com/

Troyes

The charming half-timbered houses of Troyes await eager travelers some 110 km south of Epernay. The former capital of the region makes for a great day-trip and is also known as "the town of ten churches" and the home of famous Middle Ages French writer Chrestien de Troyes. Nowadays most notably famous for its shopping outlets, it is also the proud home of a culinary specialty – the *andouillete* sausage and has rebuilt itself quite well after a devastating fire in 1524.

Troyes has spectacular churches and cathedrals and a very good Modern Art Museum. Head to the majestic Cathedral of Saint Peter and Saint Paul (*Cathedrale St-Pierre et St-Paul)* and marvel at the Flamboyant Gothic architecture and its accidental asymmetrical look with only one tower instead of two. No less than 180 stained-glass windows from multiple periods can be found in the Cathedral (Pl. St-Pierre, free entrance). Also check out the baroque organ with the musical cherubs.

The city's most famous museum is the *Musee d'Art Moderne* (Palais Épiscopal, Pl. St-Pierre, admission €5), right next to the Cathedral and housed in a 16th century bishop's palace. It hosts the private modern art collection of Pierre Levy, an industrialist and a close friend of the Fauvist painter Andre Derain whose work makes up the central part of the Museum's collection. Besides Derain, there are numerable works of art by Degas, Gauguin, Ernst and Courbet, among others.

While in Troyes, also visit the Ste-Madeleine Church – the town's oldest one – dating from the 12th century but remodelled 4 centuries later. It is mostly known for the intricate triple arch stone rood screen (one of only seven remaining in France), carved by Jean Gailde in the early 16th century.

Troyes is also an important clothing industry center and this is a sector which employs the vast majority of the town's locals. Factory outlets can be found here and designer clothes often cost just a fraction of the normal retail price. Check out the Shopping section of this guide for more information.

Recommendations for the Budget Traveller

Places to Stay

Residhome Reims Centre

6 rue de Courcelles, 51100 Reims
Tel: +33 3 26 78 17 81
http://www.residhome.com/hotel-residence-aparthotel-reims-233.html

Located in the center of Reims, the Residhome is a mere 15 minute walk from the Notre Dame Cathedral and features 76 rooms all equipped with a kitchenette. Flat-screen TVs, safety boxes and private bathrooms are all standard features found in this hotel. Breakfast is served each morning and private parking is available at a cost.

Prices for a double room at the conveniently located Residhome start at around €65 per night in September.

Sejeours & Affaires Reims Clairmarais

25 Rue Edouard Mignot, 51100 Reims
Tel: +33 3 26 07 74 63
http://www.sejours-affaires.com/hotel-residence-aparthotel-reims-177.html

Another central hotel in Reims located about 300 meters from the train station, the two-star comfortable aparthotel Sejeours & Affaires Reims Clairmarais is a good value accommodation choice in Reims. The 50 spacious apartments and studios in the complex all provide free internet access and feature a living room area as well as a kitchenette. Daily breakfast is provided on request and on-site parking is also available.

Accommodation in a double room at this excellent aparthotel starts at €70 per night during the harvest season.

Premiere Classe Epernay

Parc D'activites Val De Champagne - Boulevard Marechal
Joffre, 51200 Épernay
Tel: +33 1 73 21 98 00
http://www.premiereclasse.com/en/hotels/premiere-
classe-epernay

If you decide to base yourself in Eperney, you'll definitely
appreciate the Premiere Classe's location only a 10 minute
walk away from the town's train station. All of its 79
rooms are air-conditioned and equipped with private
bathrooms and TV.

The famous Avenue de Champagne is only 2.5 kilometers
away and beckons with its champagne houses. Rates for a
double room start at a very reasonable €50 per night
during harvest season.

La Villa Saint Pierre

1 rue Jeanne d'Arc, 51200 Épernay
Tel: +33 3 26 54 40 80
http://www.villasaintpierre.fr/

If you want to stay in a century-old townhouse in the
center of Epernay, check out the La Villa Saint Pierre – a
two start hotel with a garden and a terrace. Guest rooms
are brightly decorated and all feature private bathrooms.

Continental breakfast is available as are a-la-carte dinners.
The Villa is excellently positioned less than a kilometer
from the some of the best champagne cellars in Epernay.

Rates for one of the 14 rooms in the La Villa Saint Pierre during early fall start at around €55 per night.

Domaine du Moulin de l'Etang

Moulin de l'Etang, 51700 Châtillon-sur-Marne
Tel: +33 3 26 58 72 95
http://www.chambres-hotes.fr/chambres-hotes_domaine-du-moulin-de-l-etang_chatillon-sur-marne_25785_en.htm

If you want to base yourself away from the main two cities in Champagne and in a charming cottage right in the heart of the vineyards, check out the Domain du Moulin de l'Etang set in an 18th century building. The property has its own 5 hectare garden, a private pond and a lovely terrace and is located in Chatillon-sur-Marne, about 15 kilometers west of Epernay.

This bed and breakfast has the capacity to accommodate no more than 15 people, making it a lovely choice for those in search of tranquility and relaxation. A golf course is also available within 5 kilometers.

Standard double rooms with breakfast start at about €75 per night.

Places to Eat & Drink

La Table Anna

6 rue Gambetta, 51100 Reims
Tel: + 33 3 26 89 12 12
http://www.latableanna.fr/

The hunt for authentic and fresh French food both starts
and ends here in Reims, at the quaint but very successful
La Table Anna, located about halfway between the Notre
Dame de Reims and the St-Remi Basilica. Try the 3-course
Gourmet lunch menu (€32) or go a-la-carte; either way
dishes are rich and incredibly tasty. The family-run
restaurant has spotless service and an excellent selection
of champagnes, sold both by the glass and by the bottle.
Reservations are recommended as the place fills up
quickly with locals.

Le Bocal Restaurant

27 rue de Mars, 51100 Reims
Tel: + 33 3 26 47 02 51
http://www.restaurantlebocal.fr/

The Le Bocal is Reims' hidden gem; actually a fish shop
with only a few tables in the back, it will let you select
your preferred fresh fish or seafood and cook it to
perfection.

Try the smoked salmon dishes (from €4 per 50 grams), the impeccable oysters and the delightful salads (from €10). A surprisingly varied selection of wines (also sold by the glass) is available as are rich desserts starting from €4 in this tucked-away bistro offering excellent value in Reims.

Restaurant Chez Max

13, av AA Thevenet, Magenta, 51530 Epernay
Tel: +33 3 26 55 23 59
http://www.chez-max.com/

Chez Max (open since 1946) is one of Epernay's greatest restaurants so booking in advance is highly recommended. The popularity of the place and the loyalty of the locals is understandable given the quality of food and the various very reasonably priced fixed menus (starting from €14.50 for two courses and dessert). Don't skip the cheese boards, the delicious foie gras starter and the amazing creme brulee.

La Cave a Champagne

8 Rue Gambetta, 51200 Epernay
Tel: +33 3 26 55 50 70
http://www.la-cave-a-champagne.com/

The La Cave a Champagne is another Epernay restaurant worth booking ahead for a delightful lunch in between touring champagne houses as it provides a truly excellent-value fixed price menu for €19 (starter, main dish and dessert).

Make sure you try the scallops in champagne cream sauce and the excellent Coq au Vin. It is located in the center of Epernay, right next door to the C. Comme which beckons with a wide selection of champagnes.

Le Fille du Potager

82 Rue Urbain IV, Troyes
Tel: +33 3 25 43 12 81
http://restaurantlepotager.free.fr/

When you find yourself famished from all the shopping in Troyes, head to the Le Fille du Potager in the heart of the historic center of the city. Open year-round, it has a pleasant terrace and offers, among other dishes, the famous Troyes sausages (*andouillettes*).

Day special main dishes start at €10 (very satisfying main dish salads from €8.90) and are served by the attentive and friendly staff. Do note that there is a winding staircase leading you to the second floor of this restaurant.

Places to Shop

Vins CPH Reims

3 place Léon Bourgeois, 51100 Reims
Tel: +33 3 26 40 12 12
http://www.vinscph.com/en/node/17

Locals shop for wines in the Vins CPH where a mind-blowing selection of over 1000 varieties is offered. The range includes upwards of 150 type of champagne (ranging from €15 to €1,000 per bottle). Cognacs, whiskeys and other spirits are also on sale at the CPH where deciding what to buy may prove to be difficult.

C. Comme

8, rue Gambetta,
51200 Epernay
Tel: +33 326320955
http://www.c-comme.fr/

While in Epernay, don't skip a visit to the C.Comme, devoted entirely to the wines of the Champagne region. Over 350 champagnes can be either tasted or bought in this unique shop managed by 50 producers who have joined forces to make their products more easily available to the general public without marking up prices. The knowledgeable staff is able to make the perfect suggestion based on your preferences and Champagne-related memorabilia is sold in the store as well, making it an excellent souvenir-shopping location.

La Cloche a Fromage

19 rue St-Thibault,
51210 Epernay
Tel: +33 3 26 55 30 18
http://www.fromagerie-
tourrette.com/boutique/eperney

Cheese-fanatics should definitely visit La Cloche a Fromage, open for over a century. Founded by Rene Tourette and nowadays a chain of cheese retail stores all over France, this Epernay shop is a good choice for those on the hunt for food gifts as it stocks over 100 types of authentic French cheeses alongside deli meats and other regional products. Guided tasting tours are also organized on request.

McArthur Glen

Voie du Bois, 10150 Pont-Sainte-Marie, Troyes
Tel: +33 3 25 70 47 10
http://www.mcarthurglen.com/fr/mcarthurglen-troyes/fr/

Most visitors to Troyes don't miss the chance to visit the famous McArthur Glen, a factory-outlet store. Located some 3 kilometers northeast of the city center, it is a giant mall with over 80 shops featuring famous brands including Calvin Klein, Guess, Fossil, Hugo Boss and Swarovski, among others with most at outlet prices. This true shopping-lovers' heaven can be accessed via bus line 1 (stop Magasins). A food court and ample parking are also available on the premises.

Marques City

Rue Marc Verdier, 10150
Pont-Sainte-Marie, Troyes
Tel: + 33 9 71 27 02 66
http://www.marquescity.fr

Just near the McArthur Glen mall, Marques City – yet another coveted outlet destination – extends over nine buildings and hosts over 200 world-famous brands. It was the first mall to be created in the Pont Sainte Marie in Troyes and is still a popular destination for clothing shopping for the whole family with well-known brands selling anything from infant-wear to pret-a-porter.

Printed in Great Britain
by Amazon.co.uk, Ltd.,
Marston Gate.